What does it mean?

These old-fashioned body measurements are examples of units of measure.

Spans, digits, cubits are units for measuring distances.

The problem with using body measurements is that each human body is different. We each have different spans, paces and so on.

It is better if the units we use are all the same length.

Some things we could use are: paper clips, matchsticks, straws. These are called non-standard units for measuring distance.

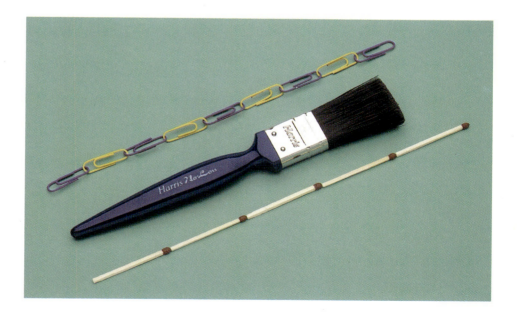

? Question

What is the length of the brush in paper clips and in matchsticks?

Measuring distance

There are lots of different types of non-standard unit for measuring distance. To make it easier to compare different distances, we all use the same units. These are called **standard units**.

For measuring short distances, we use **centimetres** and **millimetres**. We write cm and mm for short.

There are 10 millimetres in one centimetre.

10 mm = 1 cm

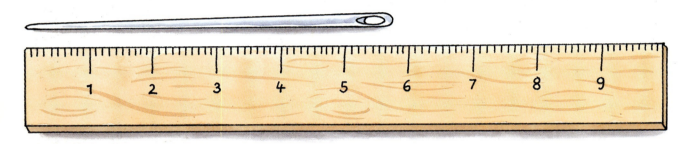

▲ *A ruler is an instrument for measuring short **lengths**.*
The needle is 5 cm and 7 mm long. We can write this as 5·7 cm.
The length of the needle is between 5 cm and 6 cm.
Its length is 6 cm, to the nearest whole centimetre.

Play the centimetre game

Use a straight edge to draw 8 straight lines. Label them A to H. Each player estimates (takes a good guess at) the length of each line to the nearest whole centimetre, and writes this down in a table. The lengths of the lines are then measured to the nearest centimetre. Find the difference between each estimate and its actual length. The winner is the player with the smallest total difference.

Line	Estimate	Length
A	5 cm	4 cm

Headfirst Into Maths

Measures

Heinemann

First published in Great Britain by Heinemann Library,
Halley Court, Jordan Hill, Oxford OX2 8EJ,
a division of Reed Educational and Professional Publishing Ltd.
Heinemann is a registered trademark of Reed Educational & Professional Publishing Limited.

OXFORD MELBOURNE AUCKLAND
JOHANNESBURG BLANTYRE GABORONE
IBADAN PORTSMOUTH NH (USA) CHICAGO

Designed by Susan Clarke
Illustrations by George Hollingworth
Origination by Ambassador Litho Ltd
Printed by Wing King Tong in Hong Kong

04 03 02 01 00
10 9 8 7 6 5 4 3 2 1

ISBN 0 431 08027 5
This title is also available in a hardback library edition (ISBN 0 431 08020 8).

British Library Cataloguing in Publication Data
Kirkby, David
Measures. – (Head first into maths)
1.Mensuration – Juvenile literature 2.Geometry –
Juvenile literature
I.Title
516.1'5

Acknowledgements
The Publishers would like to thank the following for permission to reproduce photographs:
Action Plus Photographic (Glyn Kirk), p 7; Trevor Clifford, pp 5, 11, 16, 18, 19, 26, 29; Garden &
Wildlife Matters Photo Library (J. Feltwell), p 14.

Our thanks to Hilary Koll and Steve Mills for their comments in the preparation of this book.

Every effort has been made to contact copyright holders of any material reproduced
in this book. Any omissions will be rectified in subsequent printings if notice is given
to the Publisher.

For more information about Heinemann Library books, or to order, please phone 01865 888055,
or send a fax to 01865 314091. You can visit our web site at www.heinemann.co.uk

Contents

Any words appearing in the text in bold, **like this**, are explained in the Glossary

Distance

The distance between two points is a measure of how far it is.

We often need to measure distances from one point to another.

There are different types of distance. We measure:

length to find how long something is.

width to find how wide something is.

height to find how tall something is.

depth to find how deep something is.

span

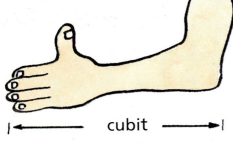
cubit

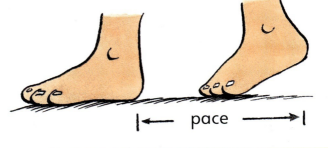
pace

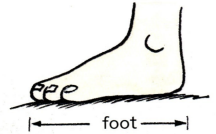
foot

▲ *Long ago, people used parts of their body to measure distances.*

Span: the distance from the thumb to the tip of the little finger across a hand when the fingers are spread out.

Cubit: the distance from the elbow to the tip of the middle finger.

Pace: the distance between the back of one heel to the back of the other heel when walking naturally.

Foot: distance from toe to heel.

Play the distance game

Choose a distance. For example, the length of the room you are in.

Estimate (make a guess at) the distance in spans, cubits and paces, and write them down. For example, length of wall: 10 paces. Then measure the distance using each of these measures. Whose estimates were the closest?

Distance	Estimate	Measure
Length of room	10 paces	11 paces

What does it mean?

For measuring longer distances, we use **metres** and **kilometres**. We write m and km for short.

There are 100 centimetres in one metre, and 100 metres in one kilometre

100 cm = 1 m

1000 m = 1 km

▼ *In most countries, distances on the road are measured in kilometres.*

motorway 8 kilometres

zoo 16 kilometres

theme park 80 kilometres

What does it mean?

Millimetres, centimetres, metres and kilometres are standard **metric units** for measuring distance. Sometimes we still use old **imperial units**, for example miles.

A mile is longer than a kilometre.

5 miles is about the same as 8 kilometres.

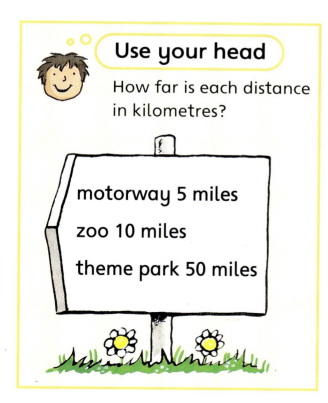

Use your head

How far is each distance in kilometres?

motorway 5 miles

zoo 10 miles

theme park 50 miles

▲ *Distances for races are usually measured in metres.*

In the Olympic Games, some of the race distances are:
100 m, 200 m, 400 m,
1500 m, 3000 m, 5000 m.

Use your head

How far are the last three races in kilometres?

Measuring weight

Weight is a measure of how heavy something is.

If it is heavy, it weighs a lot.

If it is light, it does not weigh very much.

We use a balance to compare the weights of two objects.

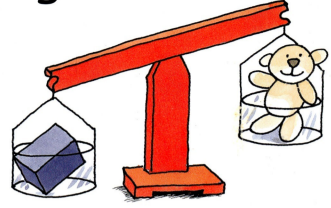

? Question
Which is the heavier, which the lighter?

To measure the weights of different objects, we use the **standard units, grams** and **kilograms**. We write g and kg for short.

There are 1000 grams in 1 kilogram.

1000g = 1 kg

▲ *These standard units can be used to find the weight of different objects. The weights have to balance the object.*

Play the kilogram game

Play this game with a friend. You need a balance, and a 1 kg weight placed on one pan.

Choose an object. You should each feel its weight, and try to estimate (make a guess) if it weighs more or less than 1 kilogram. Then test it by placing the object on the other pan. Repeat for 10 different objects. The winner is the player who makes the most correct estimates.

Cooking items are usually measured using grams.

150 g flour   50 g raisins   25 g butter

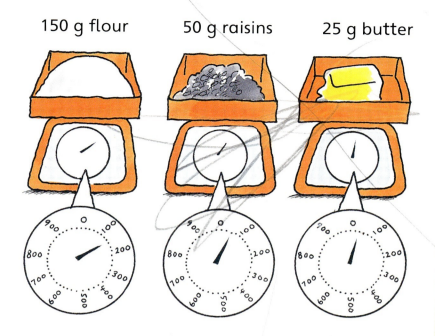

▼ *Ingredients for a recipe:*

Fruity flapjacks

Ingredients:

60 g brown sugar

125 g butter

250 g porridge oats

1 tablespoon golden syrup

100 g raisins

$\frac{1}{2}$ teaspoon salt

? Question

How much do the flour, the raisins and the butter weigh altogether?

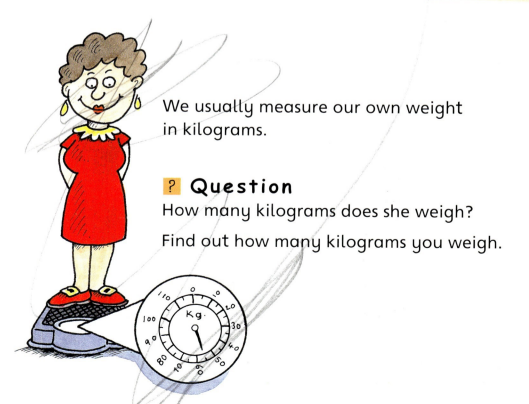

We usually measure our own weight in kilograms.

? Question

How many kilograms does she weigh?

Find out how many kilograms you weigh.

Measuring capacity

Capacity is a measure of how much a container holds.

If a bottle is filled with water, the capacity of the bottle is a measure of how much water will fill the bottle.

◀ *15 pots full of water were needed to fill the jar. The capacity of the jar is 15 pots.*

A yoghurt pot is one example of a non-standard unit of measure for capacity.

A **litre** is a **standard unit** for measuring capacity.

We write **l** for short.

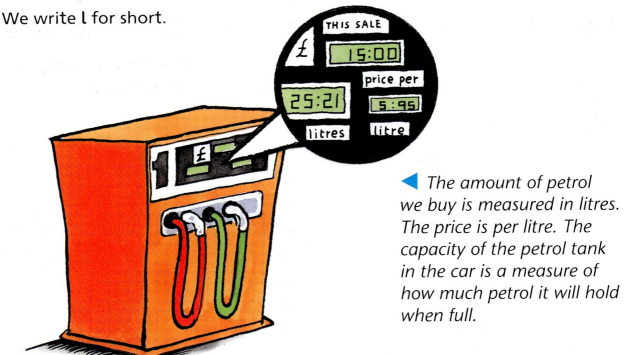

◀ *The amount of petrol we buy is measured in litres. The price is per litre. The capacity of the petrol tank in the car is a measure of how much petrol it will hold when full.*

What does it mean?

Litres are used to measure larger capacities.

Smaller capacities use **millilitres** and **centilitres** as units. We write ml and cl for short.

There are 1000 millilitres in 1 litre, and 100 centilitres in 1 litre

1000 ml = 1 l

100 cl = 1 l

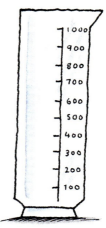

▲ *This litre measure can measure capacities in units of 100 ml.*

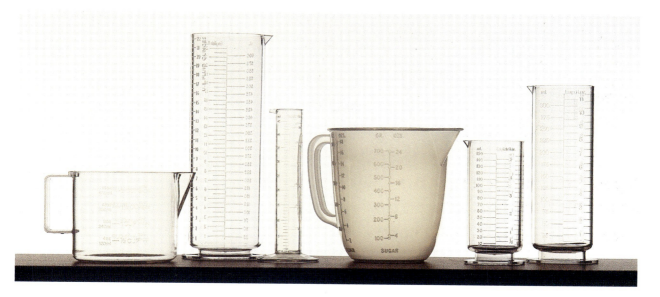

▲ *Measuring jugs and measuring cylinders are used to measure capacity.*

Use your head

Say how much liquid is in the litre measure.

Fun to do

Find some different containers in your kitchen, such as jars and bottles. Look at the labels, and write down the capacity of each container. Collect different labels.

Measuring area

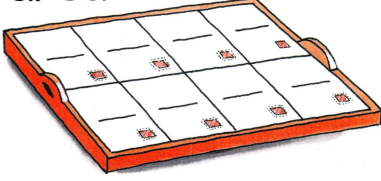

Area is a measure of how much space a flat (2-D) object covers.

❓ Question

How many postcards cover the tray?

▲ *A postcard is a non-standard unit for measuring area.*

What does it mean?

Squares fit easily together, so we use squares for **standard units** of measuring area.

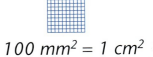

$100 \text{ mm}^2 = 1 \text{ cm}^2$

Small areas are measured using **square centimetres** and **square millimetres**. We write cm^2 and mm^2 for short.

A square centimetre is a square whose side is 1 centimetre long.

A square millimetre is a square whose side is 1 millimetre long.

▶ *You can measure the area of a handprint by counting the number of square centimetres inside the print. Count all the whole squares, then count the part squares. A sensible rule for the part squares is: if the part square is more than half a square, count it; if not, ignore it.*

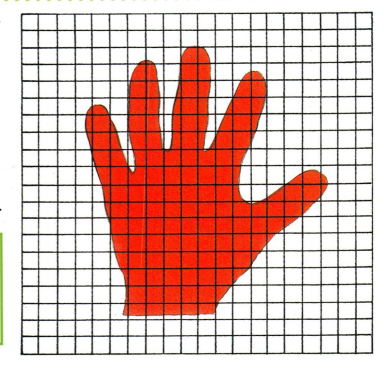

Fun to do

Find the area of your handprint and footprint.

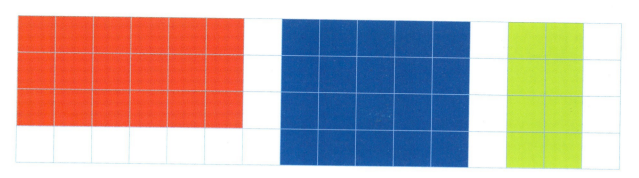

▲ *Area of red rectangle = 3 × 6 = 18 cm²*
Area of blue rectangle = 4 × 5 = 20 cm²
Area of yellow rectangle = 4 × 2 = 8 cm²
You can find the area of a rectangle by multiplying its length by its width.
Area of a rectangle = length × width.

What does it mean?

Large areas are measured using **square metres** and square kilometres. We write m² and km² for short.

A square metre is a square whose side is 1 metre long.

A square kilometre is a square whose side is 1 kilometre long.

What does it mean?

A large square whose sides are 100 metres long, has an area of 10 000 m². This unit is called a **hectare**.

The area of two football pitches is about one hectare.

Play the area game

This is a game for two players. Using centimetre squared paper, one player draws a small rectangle unseen by the other, and then counts the number of squares inside and says the area. The other player has to try to say the length and width of the rectangle. If correct, score a point. Swap roles, and play eight rounds each. The winner is the player who scores the most points.

? Question

What is the area of this garden in square metres?

Measuring perimeter

The **perimeter** of a shape is the **length** of its boundary. It is the distance all the way round the shape.

▶ *Garden fences are sold by the* **metre***. To find out how much fencing you need to buy, you need to know the perimeter of the garden to be fenced.*

In a cross-country run, you sometimes have to run the perimeter of your school playing field.

Use your head

Say the perimeter of each rectangle.

TIP 1 Double the length, double the **width**, and add these together.

TIP 2 Total one length and one width, then double this total.

Tip 1 and Tip 2 work equally well.

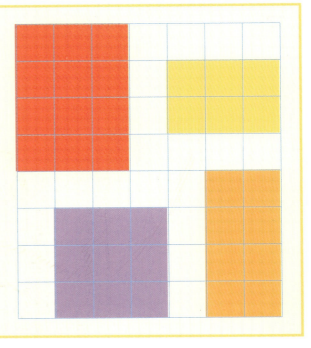

▶ *Check that each of these shapes has a perimeter of 10 units.*

Notice that each shape has the same perimeter, but they don't all have the same area.

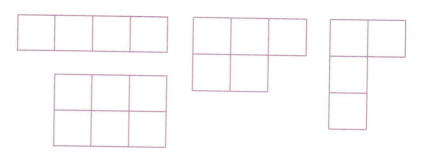

Use your head

Can you draw six different shapes on squared paper, each with a perimeter of 12 units?

? Question

Estimate the perimeters of these two shapes in **centimetres**. Now use a ruler to check how good your estimate is.

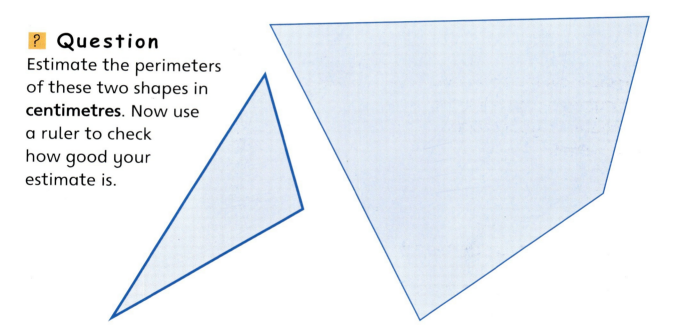

Play the perimeter game

Use a straight edge, not a ruler, to draw a triangle. Each player estimates the perimeter of the triangle in centimetres. Measure each side in centimetres and **millimetres**. Total the lengths of the three sides to find the perimeter of the triangle. Whose estimate was the closest?

Measuring volume

Volume is a measure of how much space a solid or hollow (3-D) object fills. It is sometimes confused with **capacity**.

A brick has volume because it fills space, but no capacity because it is not a container. A mug has both volume and capacity because it fills space and it is a container.

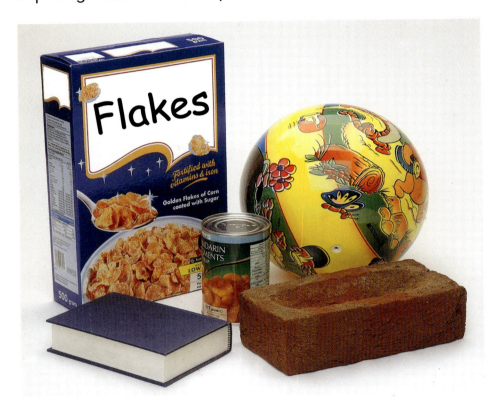

◀ *These have volume – they all fill space.*

🔲 **Question**
Which of these shapes also have capacity?

What does it mean?

Cubes fit easily together, so we use cubes for **standard units** of measuring volume.

Small volumes are measured using **cubic centimetres** and cubic **millimetres**. We write cm^3 and mm^3 for short.

A cubic centimetre is a cube whose edge is 1 centimetre long.

A cubic millimetre is a cube whose side is 1 millimetre long.

Large volumes are measured using **cubic metres**, m^3 for short.

A cubic metre is a cube whose edge is 1 metre long.

▶ This **cuboid** is built from cubic centimetres. Check that it has a **length** of 5 cm, a **width** of 3 cm and a **height** of 2 cm. The number of cubes needed for the bottom layer is 5 × 3 = 15. There are two layers, so its volume is 2 × 15 = 30 cm³.

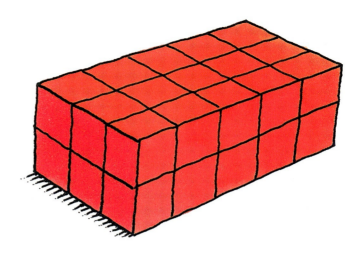

Use your head

Work out the volumes of each cuboid.

TIP Find the number of cubes on the bottom layer first.

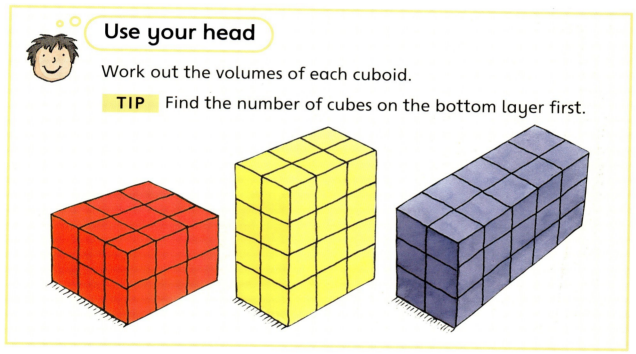

What does it mean?

This is a **litre** cube. It contains a litre of water.

The cube has an edge 10 cm long.

Its volume is 10 layers of 10 × 10 = 1000 cm³.

So, the volume of a litre of water is 1000 cm³.

Each small centimetre cube is one thousandth of 1 litre, and one thousandth of a litre is 1 **millilitre**.

So, the volume of 1 millilitre is 1 cm³.

Measuring time: hours, minutes and seconds

Clocks and watches are instruments for measuring and showing the time.

Analogue clocks and watches show the time using faces and hands.

▶ *Here are some analogue clocks.*

What does it mean?

o'clock	The minute hand points at 12.	*8 o'clock*
quarter past	The minute hand points at 3 – one quarter of the way past the hour.	*quarter past 8*
half past	The minute hand points at 6 – one half of the way past the hour.	*half past 8*
quarter to	The minute hand points at 9 – one quarter of the way towards the next hour.	*quarter to 9*
o'clock	The minute hand returns to 12, to complete one hour.	*9 o'clock*

◀ *One hour is divided into 60 minutes. Each clock number shows a block of 5 minutes.*

So, half an hour is 30 minutes and quarter of an hour is 15 minutes.

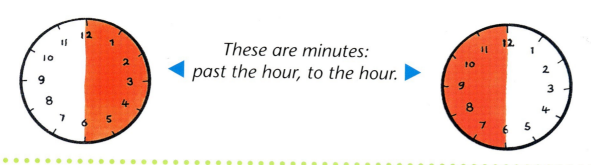

These are minutes:
past the hour, to the hour.

What does it mean?

Digital clocks and watches show the time using numbers.

▶ *The first part (before :) shows the hour, the second part (after :) shows the number of minutes past the hour.*

Use your head

Say the time on each clock or watch above.
Say how many minutes there are to go before the next hour.

▲ *A minute is divided into smaller periods of time called seconds. There are 60 seconds in 1 minute. The watch shows that it is 14 minutes (yellow hand) and 28 seconds (green hand) past 8 o'clock.*

Play the time game

This is a game for two players. You need a stopwatch set at zero. Decide on a period of time, say 25 seconds. One player holds the watch and says 'Go', the other estimates 25 seconds and says 'Stop'. Look at the watch to see how close the estimate was, and write it down. Swap roles, setting the watch at zero again. The player with the closest estimate wins the round. Play 10 rounds using different numbers of seconds to estimate. The winner is the player who wins the most rounds.

Measuring time: days

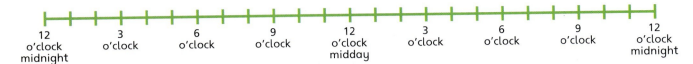

| 12 o'clock midnight | 3 o'clock | 6 o'clock | 9 o'clock | 12 o'clock midday | 3 o'clock | 6 o'clock | 9 o'clock | 12 o'clock midnight |

Each day starts at 12 o'clock midnight.

Then it is the early hours of the morning, when most people are asleep.

After waking, the morning hours move towards 12 o'clock again. This is called 12 o'clock midday (half way through the day) or 12 noon.

After 12 noon, it is called afternoon.

The day moves though the afternoon towards bedtime in the evening. Then it is back to midnight again and one day is completed. One day is 24 hours: 12 hours before midday and 12 hours after midday.

? Question

What time does the clock show?

How do we know if it is in the morning, before midday, or in the evening, after midday?

What does it mean?

To show the difference between the same time before midday and after midday, we use the letters **a.m.** and **p.m.** These are short for Latin words.

a.m. is short for *ante meridiem*, which in Latin means before midday.

p.m. is short for *post meridiem*, which in Latin means after midday.

We can write the time as 6:30 a.m. or 6:30 p.m. to show the difference between the two.

What does it mean?

Digital clocks and watches can show 24-hour time.

Using 24-hour time shows clearly the difference between before and after midday.

Since one hour after midday is the thirteenth hour of the day, the digital time is shown as 13:00.

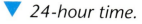

▼ *24-hour time.*

00:00   03:00   06:00   09:00   12:00   15:00   18:00   21:00   00:00

Use your head

Which of these times are before midday, and which are after?

Say each time either as an a.m. or as a p.m. time.

Measuring time: weeks, months, years

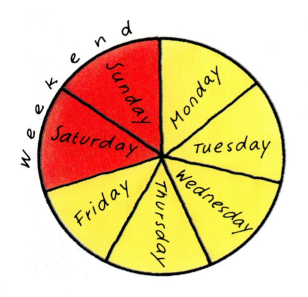

There are 7 days in a week.

Monday is the first day of the week.

Monday, Tuesday, Wednesday, Thursday and Friday are called weekdays.

Saturday and Sunday, the last two days are called the weekend (the end of the week).

2 weeks is called a fortnight, short for 14 nights.

There are 52 weeks in a year.

What does it mean?

There are 12 months in a year.

January is the first month of the year, December the last.

In this country we have four seasons:

Spring: during the months March, April and May

Summer: during the months June, July, August

Autumn: during the months September, October, November

Winter: during the months December, January and February.

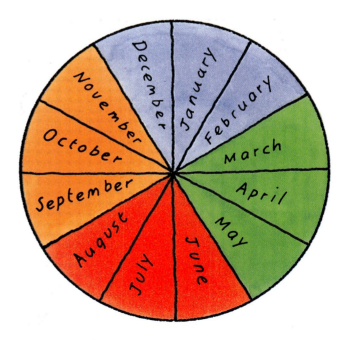

? Question

Which month is your birth month?

In which season were you born?

What does it mean?

There are 365 days in a year.

Every fourth year has 366 days – this is called a leap year.

The number of days in each month varies.

Some people remember the number of days in each month like this:

'Thirty days hath September,

April, June and November

All the rest have thirty-one,

Excepting February alone

Which hath but twenty-eight days clear

And twenty-nine in each leap year.'

Month	Days
January	31
February	28/29
March	31
April	30
May	31
June	30
July	31
August	31
September	30
October	31
November	30
December	31

▼ *A calendar month is a way of showing the different days in the month. It shows the dates of each day.*

MARCH

M	T	W	T	F	S	S
			1	2	3	4
5	6	7	8	9	10	11
12	13	14	15	16	17	18
19	20	21	22	23	24	25
26	27	28	29	30	31	

Use your head

On what day is the first and last day of the month?

Say how many Mondays there are in this month. Say how many there are of each of the other days of the week.

What does it mean?

A century is a period of 100 years.

A millenium is a period of 1000 years.

The year 856 is in the ninth period of 100 years which is called the 9th century.

The year 1999 is in the 20th century.

The first day of January 2000 is an important date because it is the first day of a millenium, and the first day of the 21st century. The years 2000, 2001, … are at the beginning of a new millenium.

Timetables

A timetable is a quick way of showing lots of information easily.

It is a table showing times when things will happen.

A bus timetable shows the times that buses will arrive at different bus stops.

Bus Station	07:50	08:50	10:50	11:50	13:50	14:50	16:50	18:00
Long Manor	07:57	08:57	10:57	11:57	13:57	14:57	16:57	18:07
Village Market	08:01	09:01	11:01	12:01	14:01	15:01	17:01	18:10
Village Church	08:05	09:05	11:05	12:05	14:05	15:05	17:05	18:14
Railway Station	08:08	09:08	11:08	12:08	14:08	15:08	17:08	18:16
York Hotel	08:11	09:11	11:11	12:11	14:11	15:11	17:11	18:19
Crossroads	08:13	09:13	11:13	12:13	14:13	15:13	17:13	18:21
St Mary's Church	08:20	09:20	11:20	12:20	14:20	15:20	17:20	18:27
Crystal Peaks	08:31	09:28	11:28	12:28	14:28	15:28	17:28	18:35
Bus Station	08:37	09:34	11:34	12:34	14:34	15:34	17:34	18:41

Use your head

Say the time taken by the bus between each pair of bus stops.

Which bus will you get to be at the York Hotel for quarter past two in the afternoon?

▲ *Check that there are 8 buses each day.*

❓ Question

What time does the last bus leave the bus station?

What time does it return to the station?

How long does the whole journey take?

A cinema timetable shows you when the week's films are showing, how often they are shown each day, and how long the film lasts.

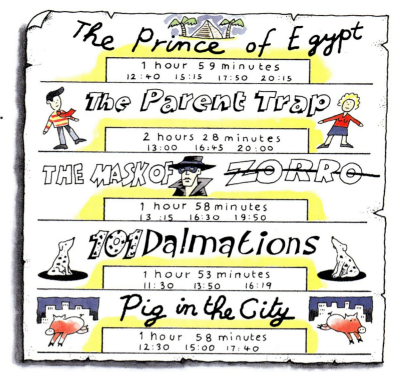

The Prince of Egypt
1 hour 59 minutes
12:40 15:15 17:50 20:15

The Parent Trap
2 hours 28 minutes
13:00 16:45 20:00

THE MASK OF ZORRO
1 hour 58 minutes
13:15 16:30 19:50

101 Dalmations
1 hour 53 minutes
11:30 13:50 16:19

Pig in the City
1 hour 58 minutes
12:30 15:00 17:40

? Question

What is the shortest film?

How many times is each film shown in a day?

Use your head

Say the starting time of each film as an a.m. or p.m. time.

A flight timetable shows the times of all the flights from one place to another. For example, this timetable shows the flights from London Heathrow to Manchester in a week.

Heathrow → Manchester

Flight No	Frequency	Depart	Arrive
BD580	Mon–Sun	06:55	07:50
BD582	Mon–Sun	07:50	08:45
BD584	Mon–Sun	09:15	10:10
BD586	Mon–Fri	10:45	11:40
BD586	Sat–Sun	11:10	12:05
BD588	Mon–Fri	12:45	13:40
BD590	Mon–Sun	17:15	18:10
BD592	Mon–Sun	18:20	19:15
BD594	Mon–Sun	20:40	21:30

? Question

How many flights are there for each day of the week?

Circles

A circle is a flat shape whose side is perfectly round.

It has a centre. Each part of the boundary of the circle is the same distance from its centre.

This distance is called its **radius**.

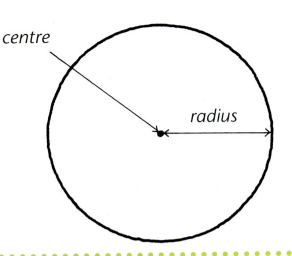

What does it mean?

If an object is shaped like a circle it is called circular.

Half a circle is called a semicircle.

Quarter of a circle is called a quarter-circle.

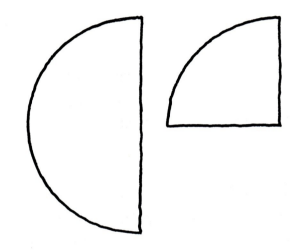

◀ *Circles appear in objects all around us.*

There are different ways of drawing a circle.

METHOD 1 Draw round an object, for example a lid.

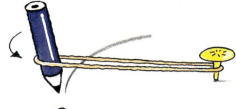

METHOD 2 Attach some cord/string to a drawing pin at one end and a pencil at the other end. Keep the drawing pin fixed and the string tight, and draw the circle with the pencil.

METHOD 3 Use an instrument especially made for drawing circles, called a pair of compasses.

What does it mean?

The **length** of a straight line drawn from one side of the circle to the other, passing through the centre is called its **diameter**.

The diameter is twice the length of the radius.

The distance around the curved boundary of a circle is called its **circumference**.

To measure the circumference of a circle, use a piece of cotton, and wrap it round the boundary as accurately as you can. Mark the distance on the cotton. The cotton is then stretched tight, and placed alongside a ruler or tape measure so that its length can be measured.

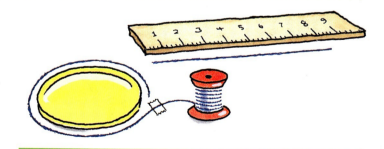

Fun to do

Find some circles, and measure their circumferences.

Angles

When two straight lines meet they form an **angle**.

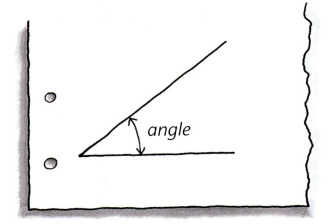

The size of the angle is measured by the amount of turn from the direction of one line to the direction of the other.

These angles are of different sizes. Which do you think is the largest and which is the smallest angle?

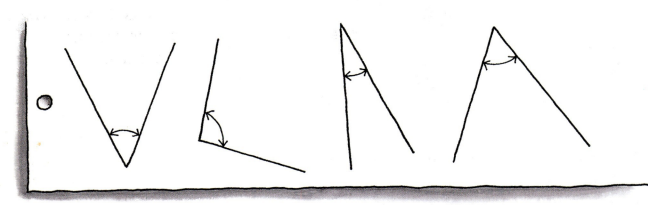

An angle which is exactly one quarter of a whole turn is called a right-angle. A right-angle can be divided into smaller angles, measured in **degrees**. There are 90 degrees in a right-angle. We write the symbol, °, to mean degrees.

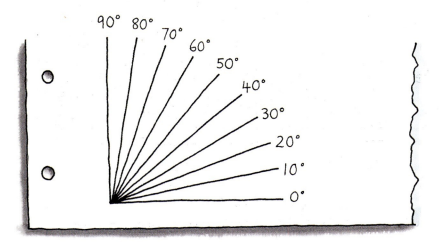

What does it mean?

A **protractor** is an instrument for measuring the size of an angle.

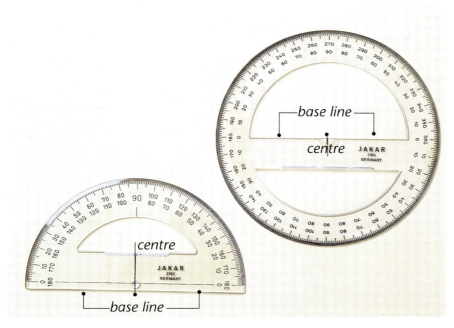

◀ *There are two types of protractor: a 180° or semicircular protractor and a 360° or circular protractor. Each has a base line and a centre point. Each has two scales: an inside scale and an outside scale which read in opposite directions.*

To measure an angle, place the centre of the protractor on the meeting point of the lines which make the angle. then line the base line up with one of the arms of the angle. Choose the scale for which this arm points at 0°, and read the position of the other arm on this scale.

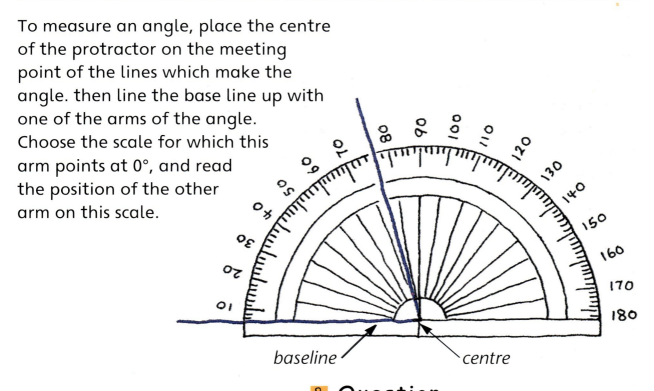

? Question

What size is this measured angle?

Glossary

analogue clock	clock which shows the time using a face and hands
angle	amount of turn from one line where it is joined to another
a.m.	times between midnight and midday; stands for *ante meridiem* which is Latin for 'before midday'
area	the amount of surface covered by a two-dimensional shape
capacity	a measure of the greatest amount which a container can hold
centilitre	unit for measuring capacity; one hundred centilitres are the same as one litre
centimetre	unit for measuring length; one hundred centimetres is the same as one metre
circumference	the distance around a circle
cube	three-dimensional shape which has six square faces all the same
cuboid	three-dimensional shape which has six rectangular faces
cubic centimetre	unit for measuring volume; a cube whose edges are one centimetre long
cubic metre	unit for measuring volume; a cube whose edges are one metre long
degree	unit for measuring angle
depth	measure of how far it is from the top to the bottom of something
diameter	distance across a circle, passing through the centre
digital clock	clock which shows the time using digits or numbers
gram	metric unit for measuring weight
hectare	unit for measuring large areas; one hectare is ten thousand square metres
height	measure of how tall or how high something is
imperial units	old units of measure which are not metric, e.g. miles, yards, ounces

kilogram	metric unit for measuring weight; one kilogram is one thousand grams
kilometre	metric unit for measuring length and distance; one kilometre is one thousand metres
length	measure of the distance of something from one end to the other
litre	metric unit for measuring capacity and volume
metre	metric unit for measuring length and distance; one metre is one hundred centimetres
metric unit	units of measure which are related by multiples of 10, 100, 1000, ..., e.g. millimetres, centimetres, metres, kilometres
millilitre	metric unit for measuring capacity; one thousand milliltres are the same as one litre
millimetre	unit for measuring length; ten milliltres is the same as one centimetre
perimeter	the distance all around the boundary of a shape
protractor	an instrument for measuring angles; used to find how many degrees are in an angle
p.m.	times between midday and midnight; stands for *post meridiem* which is Latin for 'after midday'
radius	the distance from the centre of a circle to its boundary
square centimetre	metric unit for measuring area; a square whose sides are one centimetre long
square metre	metric unit for measuring area; a square whose sides are one metre long
square millimetre	metric unit for measuring area; a square whose sides are one millimetre long
standard unit	measuring unit in common use, e.g. metres
volume	the amount of space a 3-D shape takes up
weight	a measure of how heavy or light something is
width	a measure of the distance across something from side to side

Answers

Page 5
Question 8 paper clips, $4\frac{1}{2}$ matchsticks

Page 7
Use your head
5 miles = 8 kilometres,
10 miles = 16 kilometres,
50 miles = 80 kilometres
Use your head
1500 m = 1·5 kilometres,
3000 m = 3 kilometres,
5000 m = 5 kilometres

Page 8
Question The brick is heavier.
The teddy is lighter.

Page 9
Question 225 grams

Page 11
Use your head 400 ml

Page 12
Question 8 postcards

Page 13
Question 70 m^2

Page 14
Use your head
colour: 14 cm, colour: 10 cm,
colour: 12 cm, colour: 12 cm

Page 15
Use your head
Some examples include:

Question triangle: 18 cm;
quadrilateral: 30 cm

Page 16
Question cereal box, can

Page 17
Use your head
18 cm^3, 24 cm^3, 30 cm^3

Page 19
Use your head
ten past seven, ten to four,
twenty eight minutes past four,
seventeen minutes to six;
50 minutes, 10 minutes,
32 minutes, 17 minutes

Page 20
Question 6:30; we do not know

Page 21
Use your head
A 2:55 p.m., B 12:49 p.m.,
C 8:18 p.m., D 7:15 a.m.
E 5:46 a.m., F 9:25 a.m.

Page 22
Question pupil's own answer

Page 23
Use your head
First day: Thursday
Last day: Saturday
Mondays, 4 Tuesdays, 4
Wednesdays, 4 Thursdays, 5
Fridays, 5 Saturdays, 5 Sundays, 4

Page 24
Use your head
Bus station to Long Manor:
7 minutes, Long Manor to Village
Market: 4 minutes, Village
Market to Village Church:
4 minutes, Village Church to
Railway Station: 3 minutes,
Railway Station to York Hotel:
3 minutes, York Hotel to
Crossroads: 2 minutes, Crossroads
to St Mary's Church: 7 minutes,
St Mary's Church to Crystal
Peaks: 11 minutes, Crystal Peaks
to Bus Station: 6 minutes
13:50 bus from Bus Station
Question
18:00, 18:41; 41 minutes

Page 25
Question
101 Dalmations. Each film is
shown 3 times except The Prince
of Egypt: 4 times
Use your head
12:40 p.m.; 3:15 p.m., 5:50 p.m.,
8:15 p.m.; 1:00 p.m., 4:45p.m.,
8:00 p.m.; 1:15 p.m., 4:30 p.m.,
7:50 p.m.; 11:30 a.m., 1:50 p.m.,
4:10 p.m.; 12:30 p.m., 3:00 p.m.,
5:40 p.m.
Question
Monday: 8, Tuesday: 8
Wednesday: 8, Thursday: 8,
Friday: 8, Saturday: 7, Sunday: 7

Page 29
Question 78°

Index